T0087872

WORLD'S FAVORITE

BEST

KNOWN

DEBUSSY

PIANO MUSIC

COMPILED BY

ALEXANDER SHEALY

FOREWORD

This volume includes most of the world famous piano compositions of the immortal CLAUDE DEBUSSY. Each selection is COMPLETE and in its ORIGINAL FORM.

Here you will find the everlasting charm of "Clair de Lune," "Reverie," "The Afternoon Of A Faun," as well as Debussy's brilliant suites for the piano, including "Pour Le Piano," "Estampes, "Bergamesque" and "Images."

This collection of Debussy piano music will forever remain a treasure in your music library.

The Publisher

ASHLEY
PUBLICATIONS
Distributed by
Hal Leonard

CLAUDE DEBUSSY

BORN ST. GERMAIN-EN-LAYE (NEAR PARIS)
AUGUST 22, 1862
DIED PARIS, FRANCE, MARCH 25, 1918

Debussy was admitted to the Paris Conservatory at age 11, where he studied for about 10 years. Shortly thereafter, he won the coveted "Prix de Rome" for a cantata "The Prodigal Infant." A few years later, his opera "Pelleas et Melisande" attracted world wide recognition.

Debussy's music is regarded as "ultra-modernistic." His elegant piano suites have won an important place among the world's greatest music literature. Lavishly praised for his originality of concept is his album "The Children's Corner," written especially for his daughter, Chou-Chou. Debussy's works have affected the direction of modern composers all over the world and have become an important part of the world's cultural heritage.

Debussy's orchestral works gave new dimensions to the orchestra, opening a new field of technique with astounding new theories in the complex world of harmony, melody and rhythm.

At the age of 55, this great master of music died of cancer during the bombardment of Paris in 1918 by the Germans.

CONTENTS

FIRST ARABESQUE

CLAUDE DEBUSSY

Tempo rubato *(un peu moins vite) (somewhat slower)*

SECOND ARABESQUE

CLAUDE DEBUSSY

Allegretto scherzando (playfully and lightly)

PRELUDE

From "Suite Bergamasque"

CLAUDE DEBUSSY

Moderato *(tempo rubato)*

CLAIR DE LUNE

(Moonlight)
From "Suite Bergamasque"

CLAUDE DEBUSSY

Andante *très expressif* (slow, with much expression)

pp morendo jusqu'à la fin (gradually softer to the end)

PASSEPIED
From "Suite Bergamasque"

CLAUDE DEBUSSY

Allegretto ma non troppo   (moderately fast)

BALLADE

CLAUDE DEBUSSY

Animez peu à peu

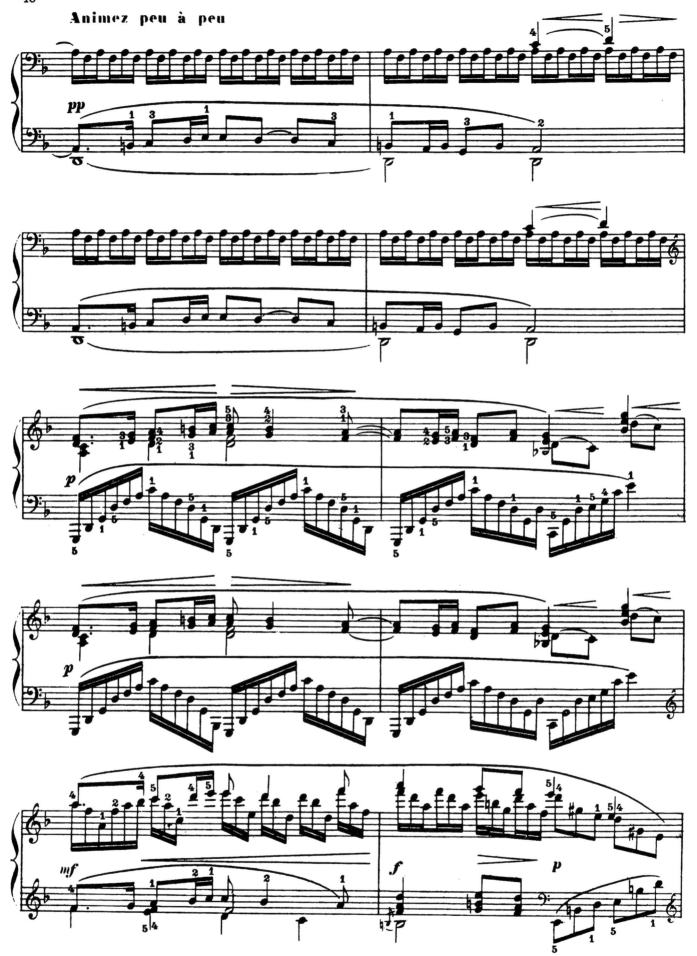

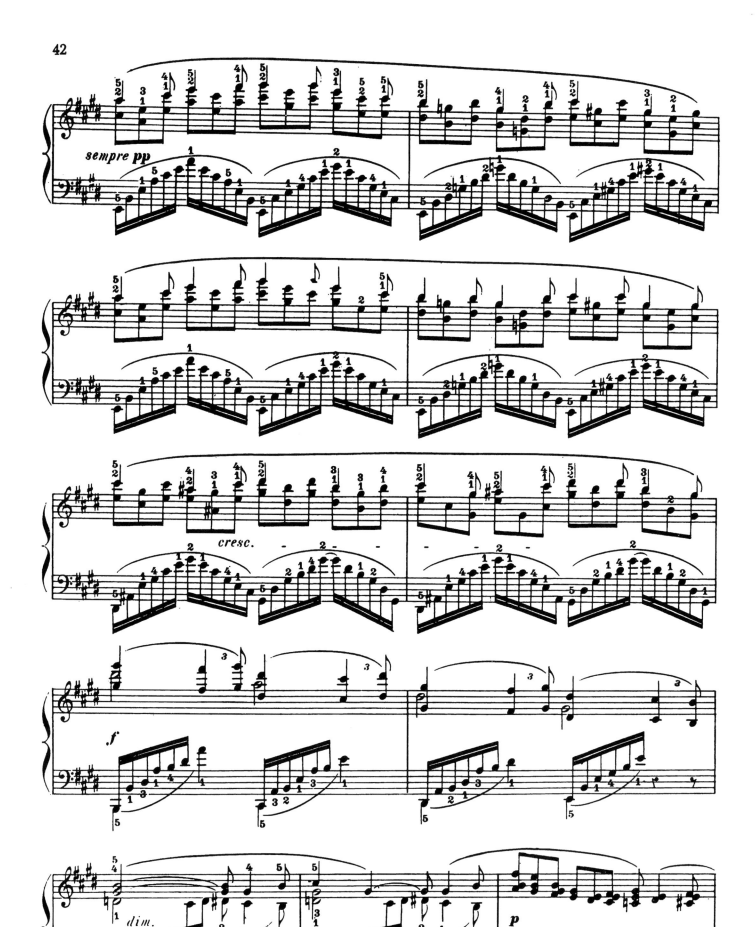

Le Cahier d'Esquisses

CLAUDE DEBUSSY
(1903)

REVERIE

CLAUDE DEBUSSY

PRELUDE
From "Pour Le Piano"

CLAUDE DEBUSSY

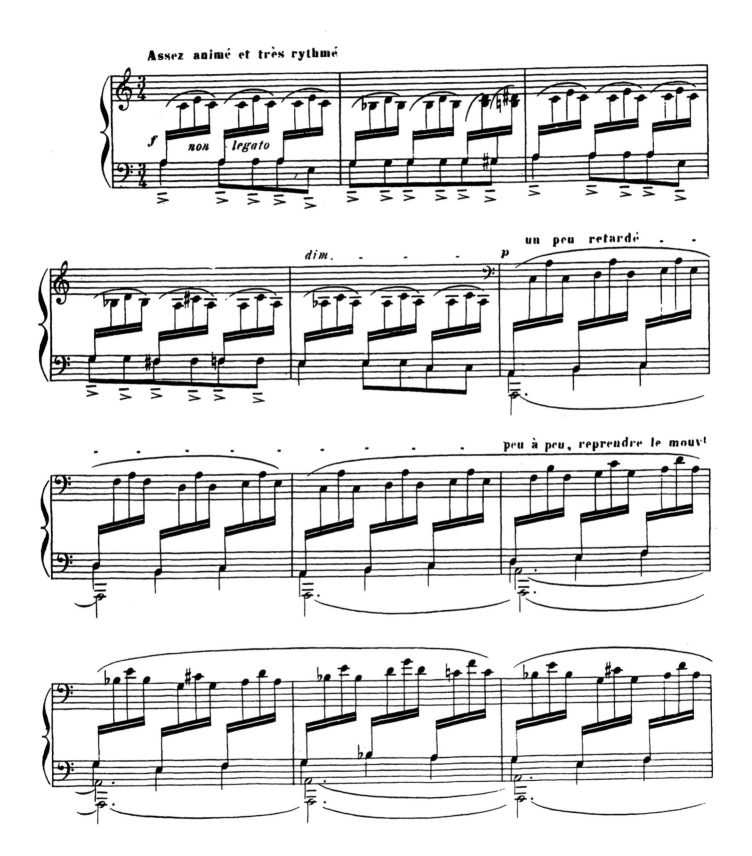

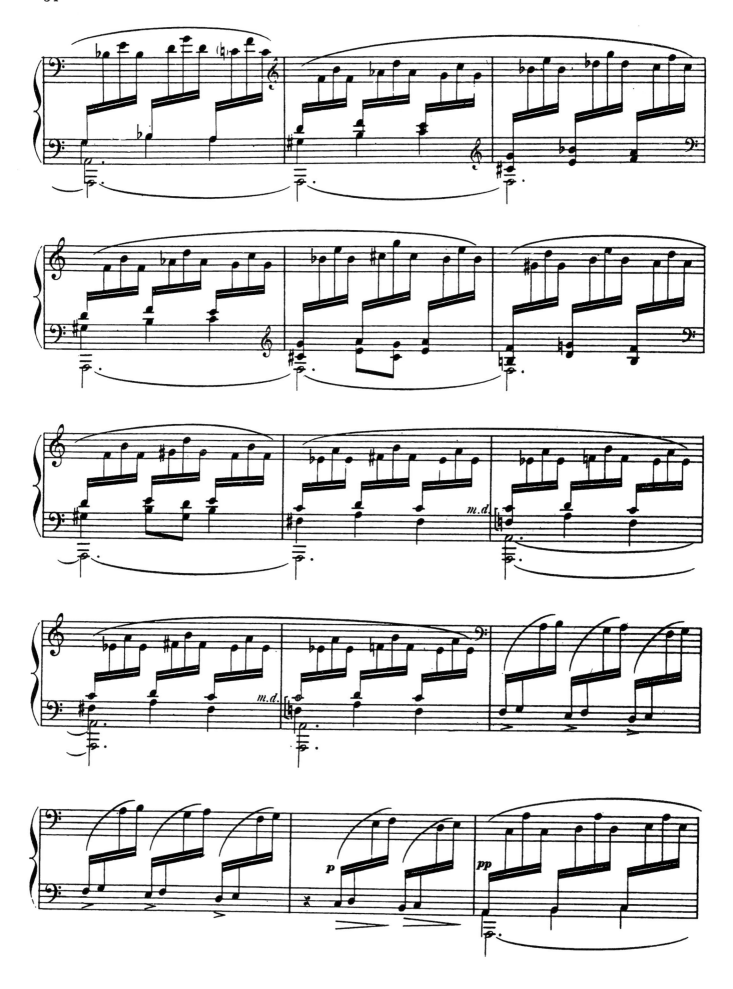

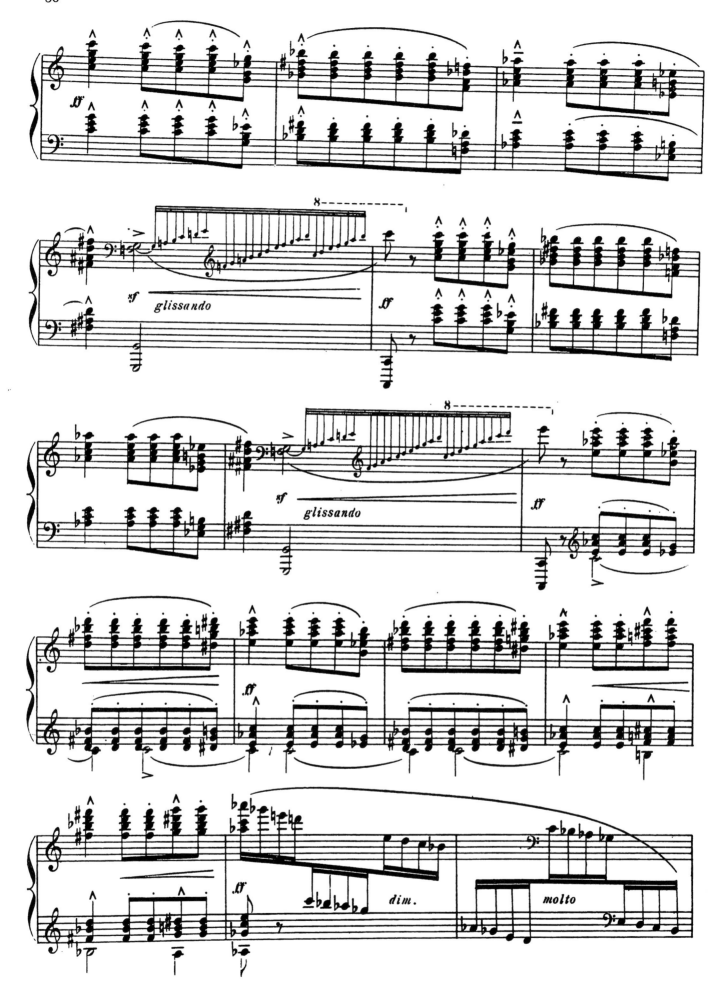

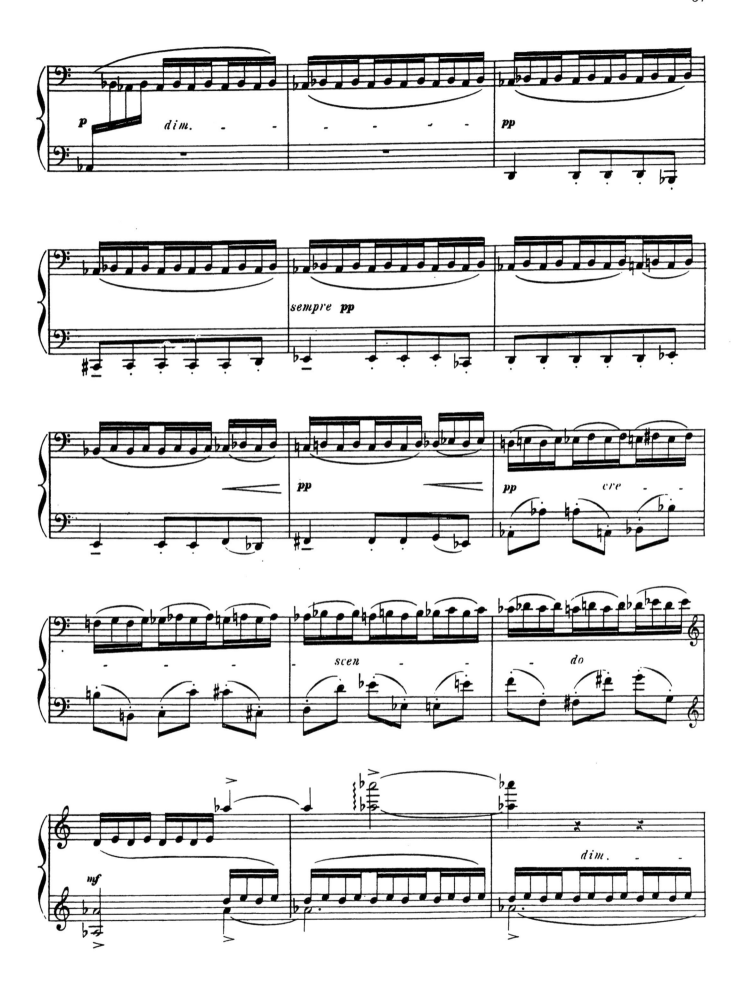

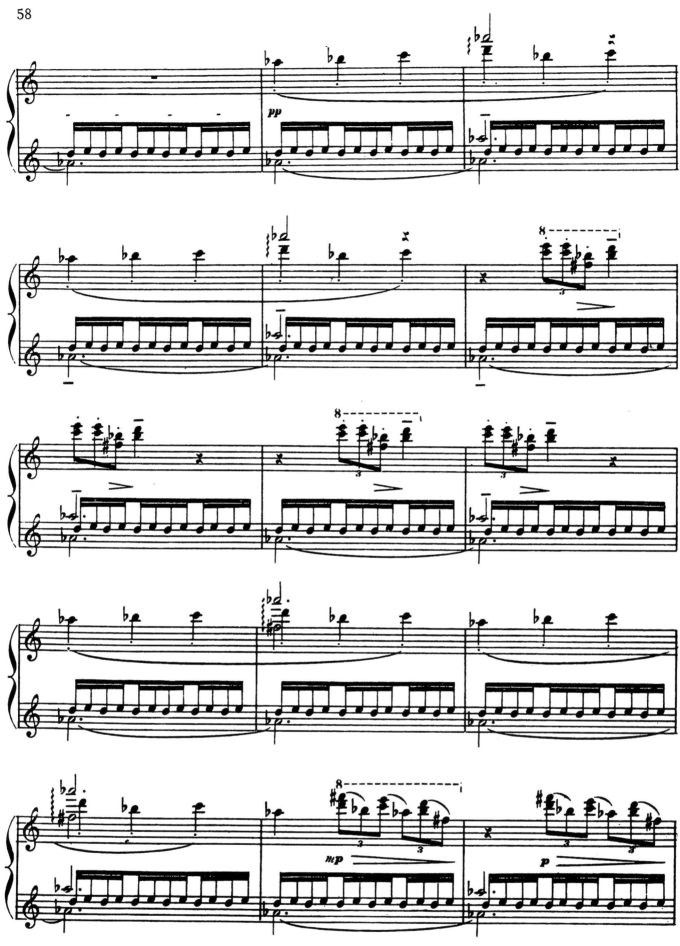

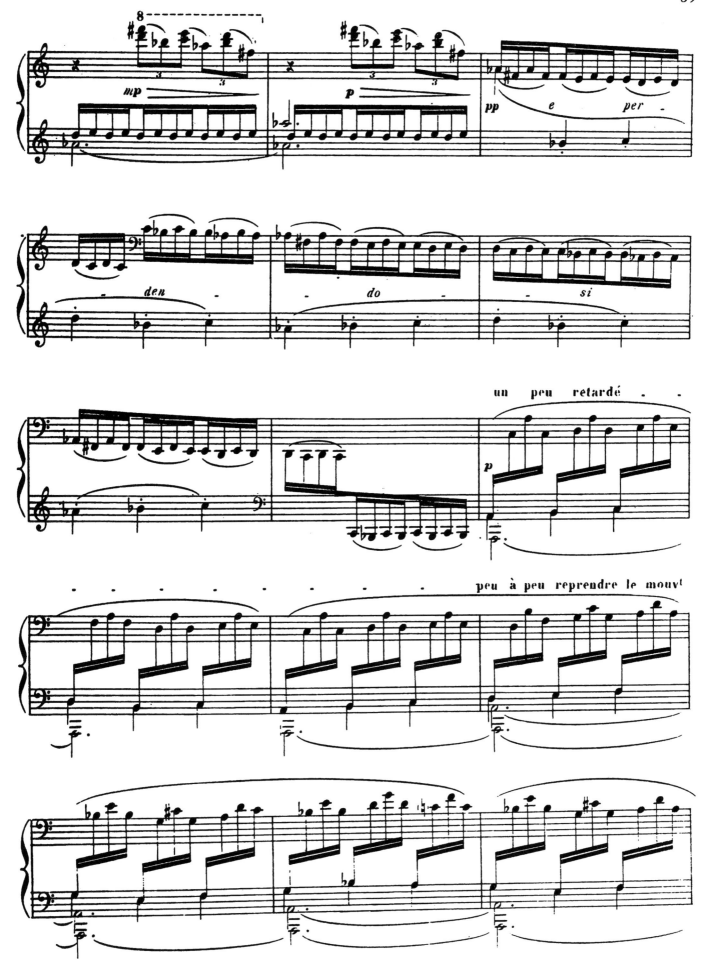

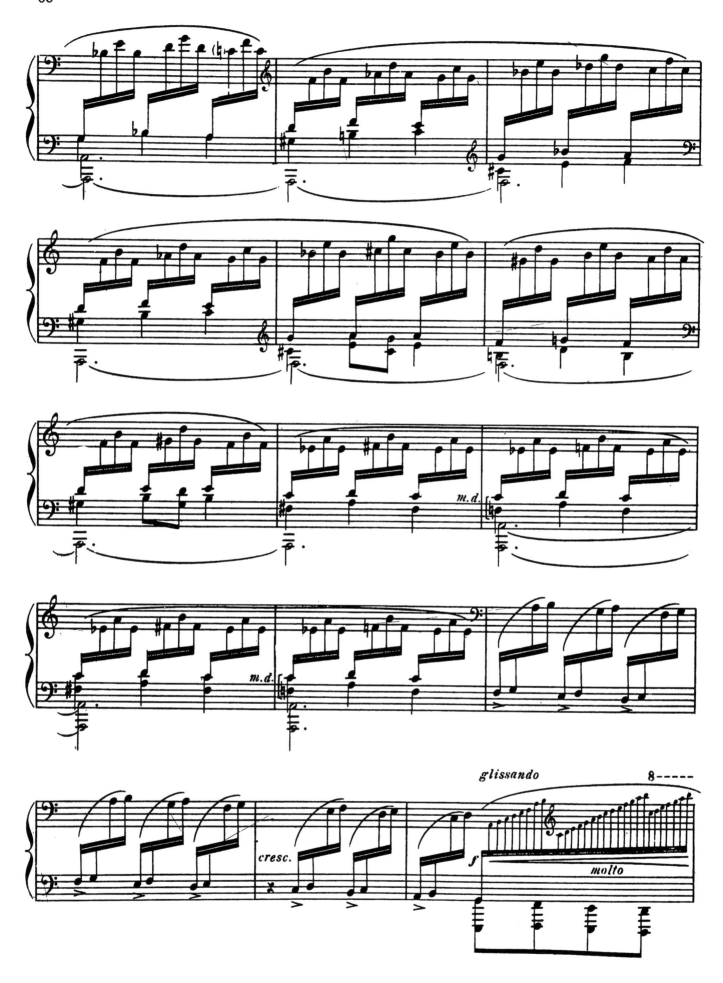

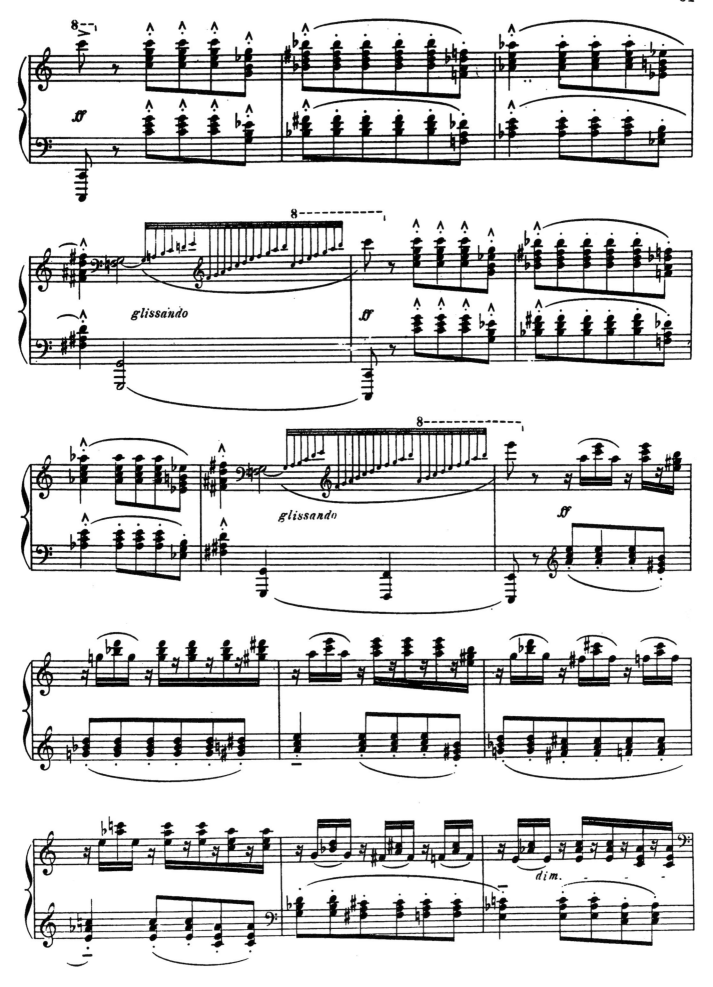

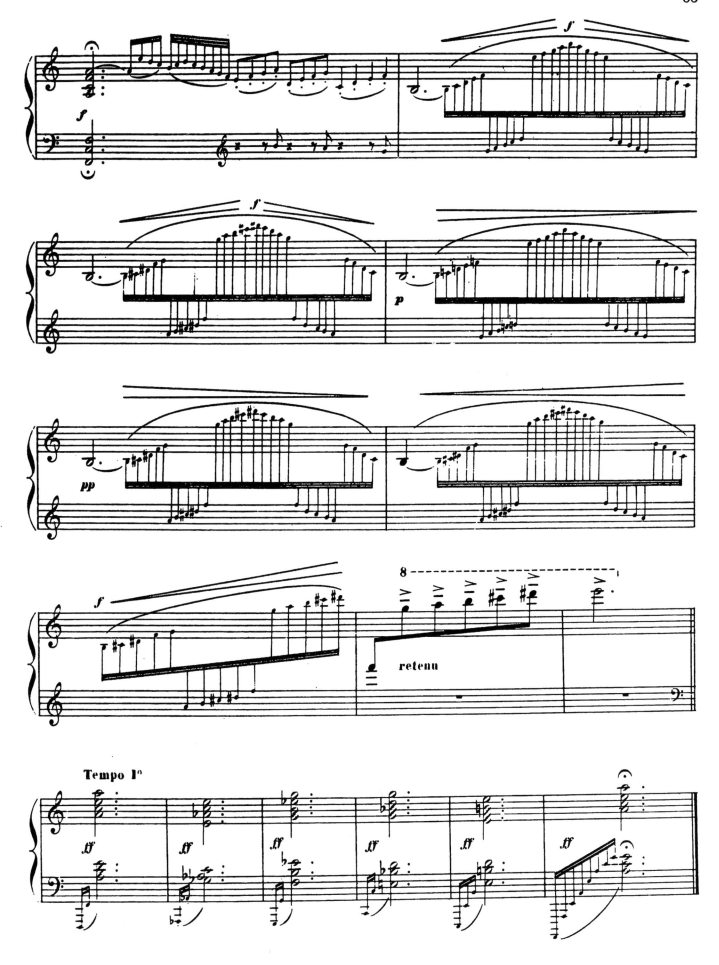

SARABANDE

From "Pour Le Piano"

CLAUDE DEBUSSY

Avec une élégance grave et lente (with a slow and solemn elegance)

TOCCATA
From "Pour Le Piano"

CLAUDE DEBUSSY

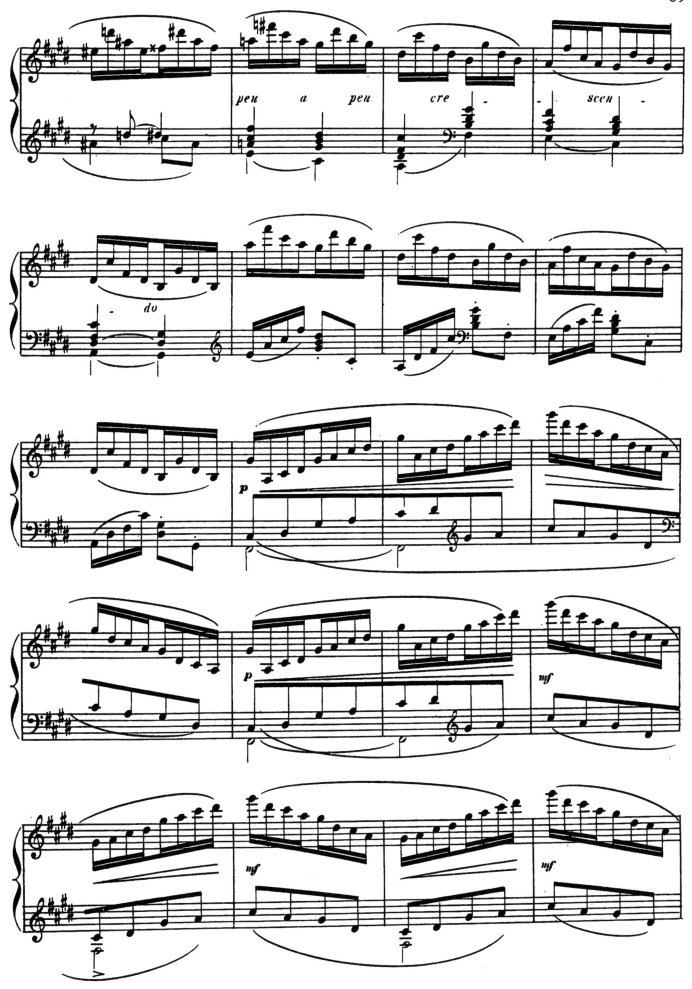

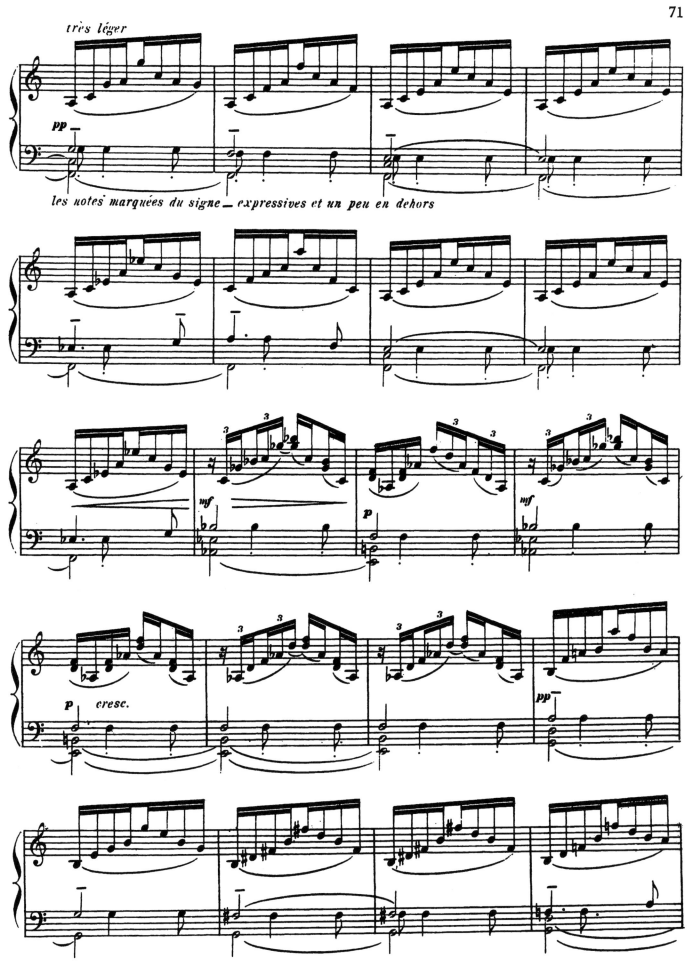

PAGODES

From "Estampes"

CLAUDE DEBUSSY

Revenez au 1º Tempo

dans une sonorité plus claire

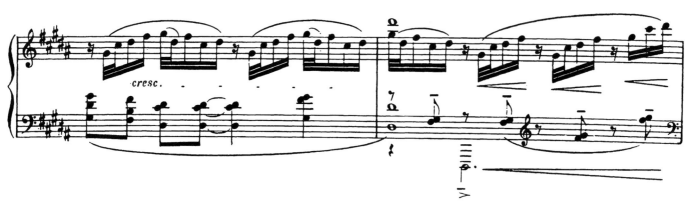

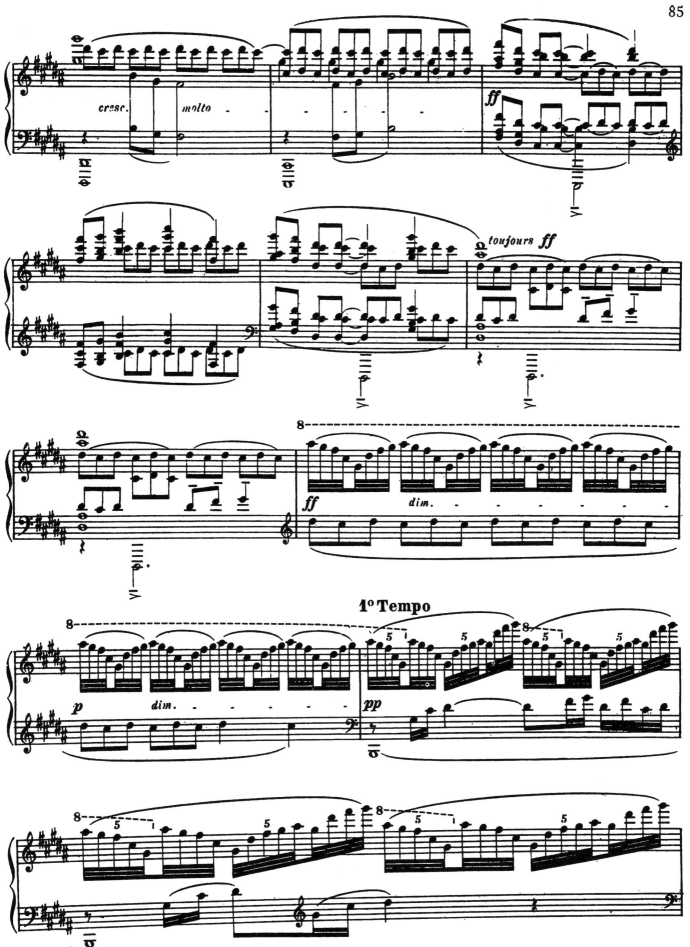

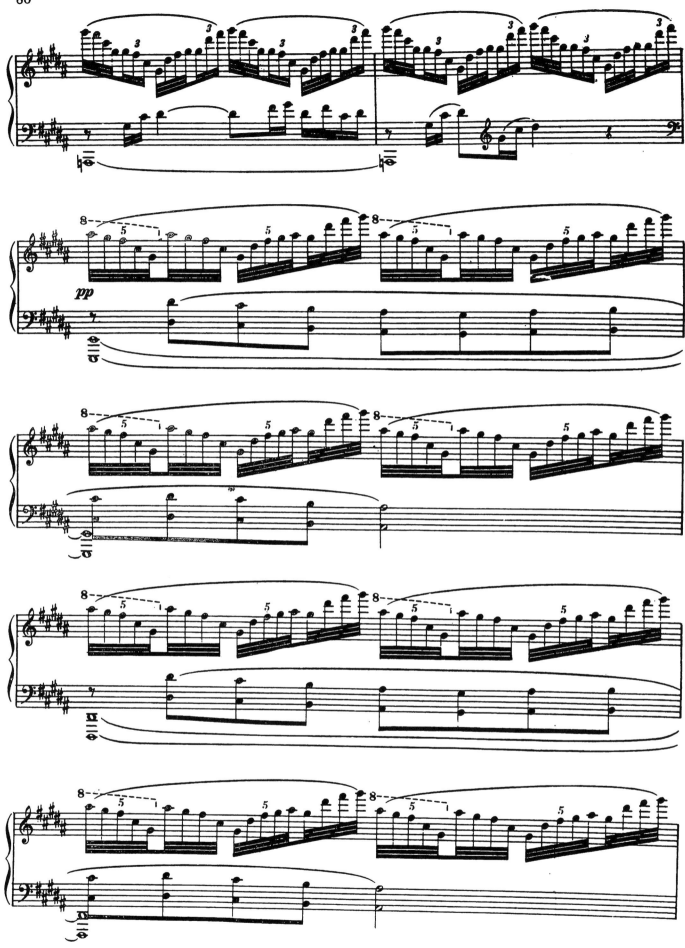

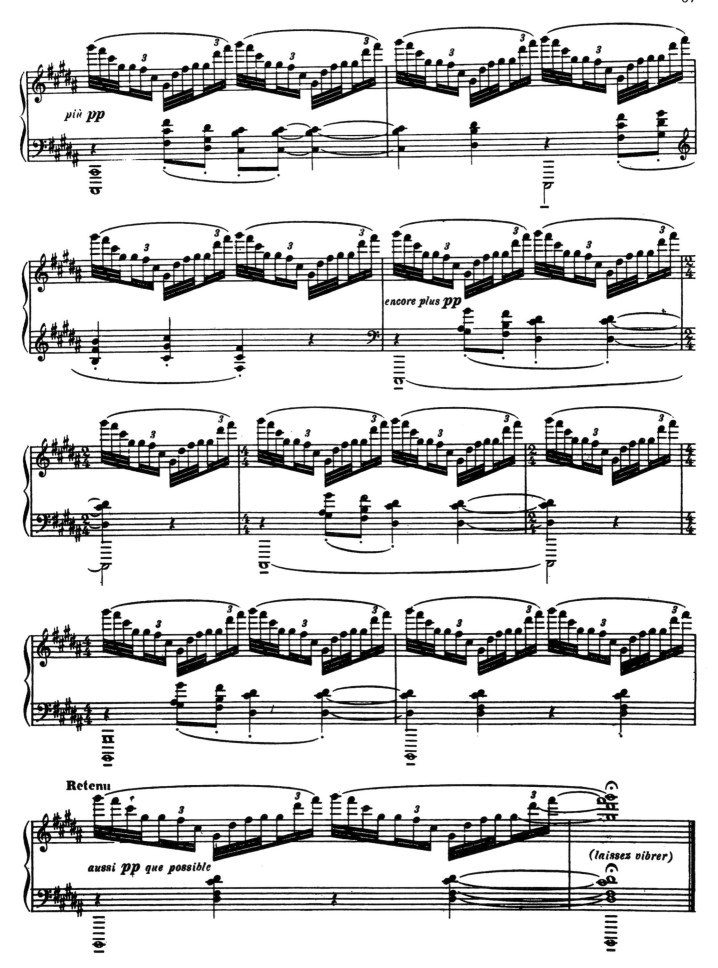

LA SOIREE DANS GRENADE

(Evening In Grenada)
From "Estampcs"

CLAUDE DEBUSSY

Mouvement de Habanera
Commencer lentement dans un rythme nonchalamment gracieux
Begin slow with graceful, nonchalant rhythm

Léger et lointain

Tempo I°

Tempo I°

JARDINS SOUS LA PLUIE

(Gardens In The Rain)
From "Estampes"

CLAUDE DEBUSSY

Net et vif (distinctly and rapidly)

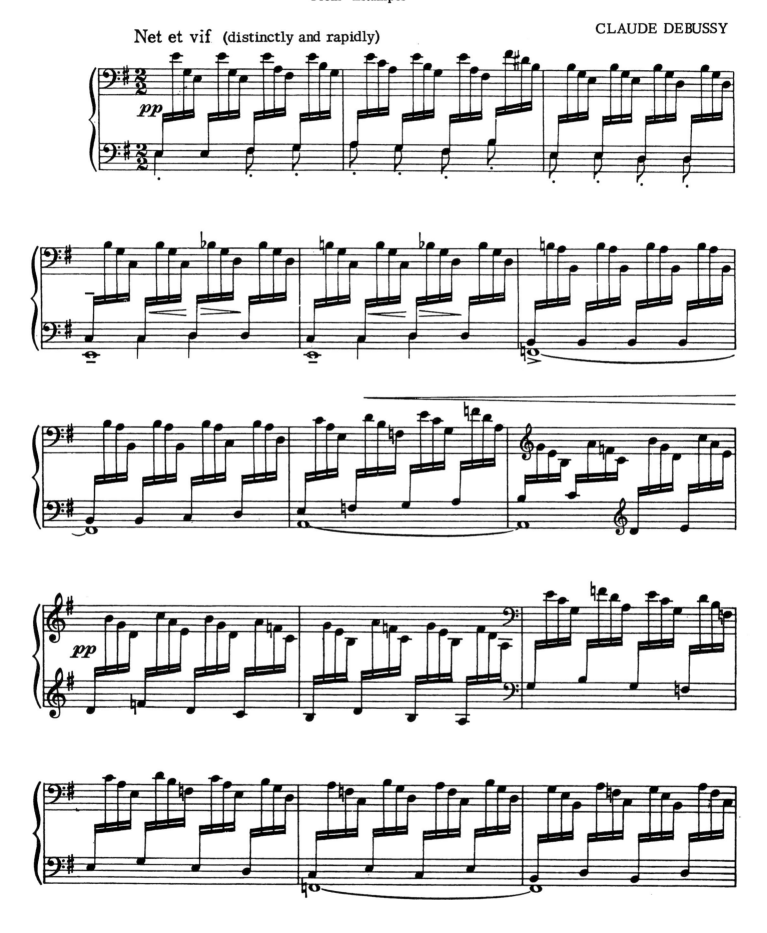

98

REFLETS DANS L'EAU

(Reflections In The Water)
From "Images"

Andantino molto (tempo rubato)

CLAUDE DEBUSSY

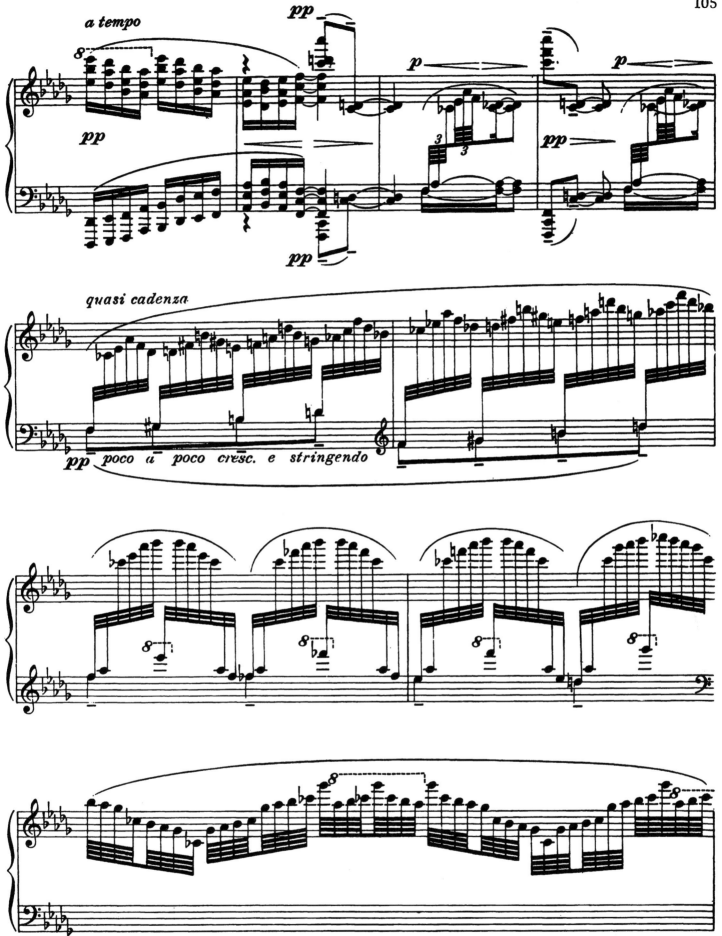

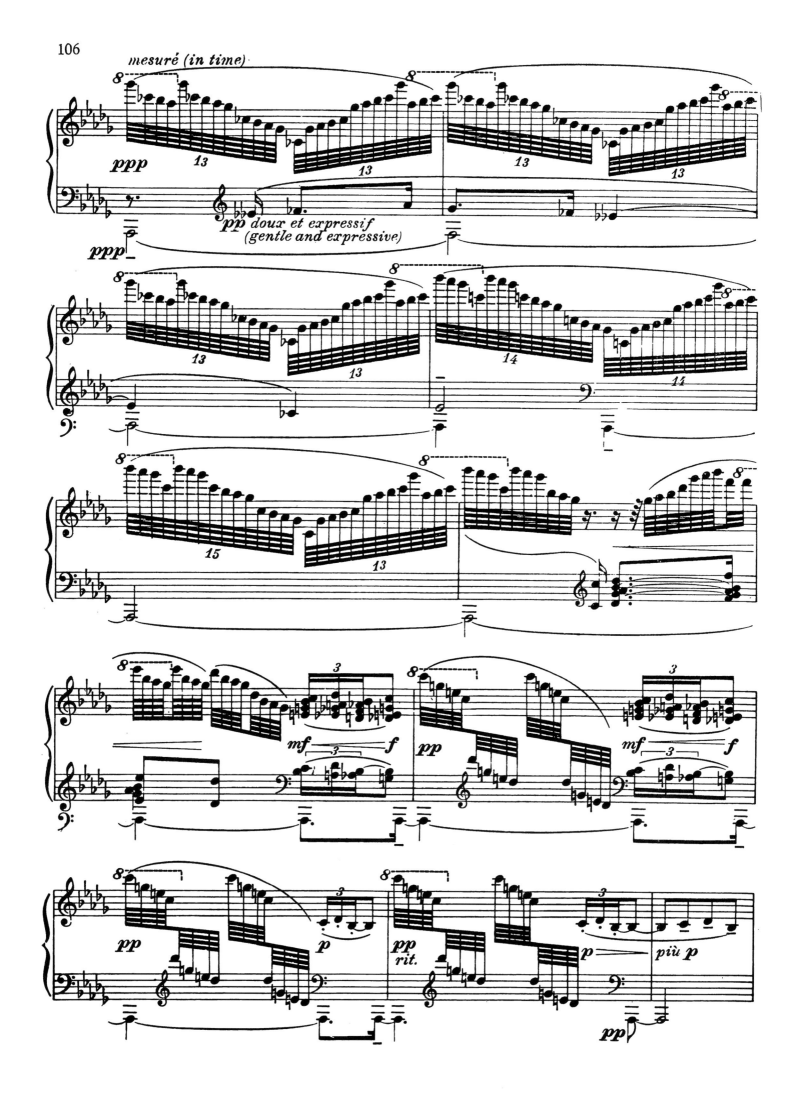

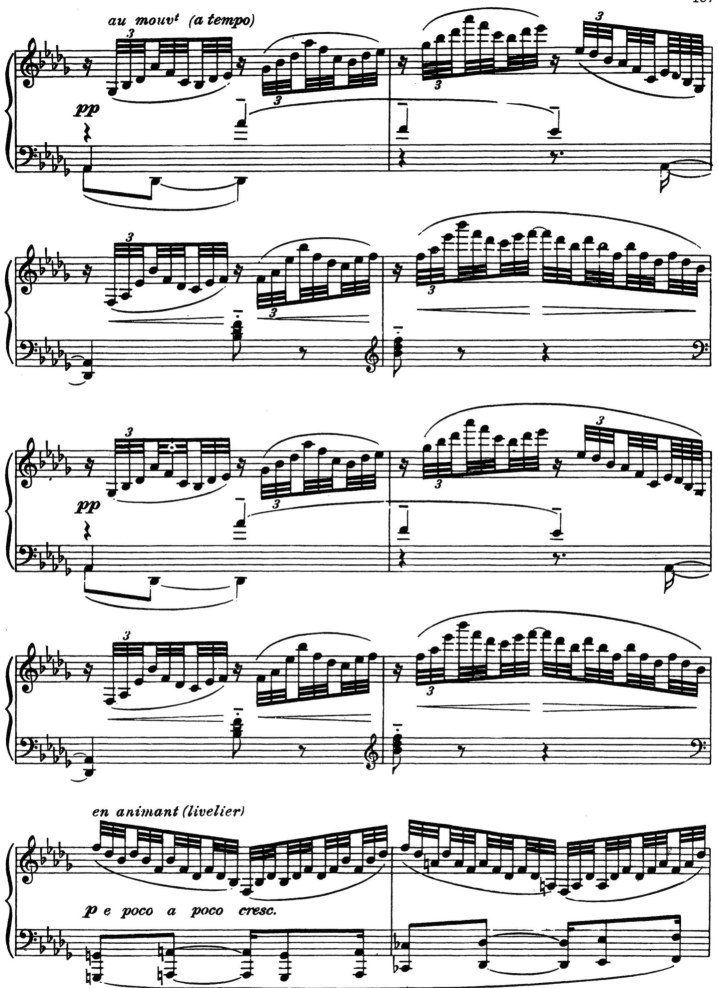

Lent *(Slowly)*
(dans une sonorité harmo-
(with an harmonious and

rit.

un peu en dehors (slightly marked)

nieuse et lointaine)
remote sounding sonority)

MOUVEMENT

Animé (avec une légèreté fantasque mais précise)

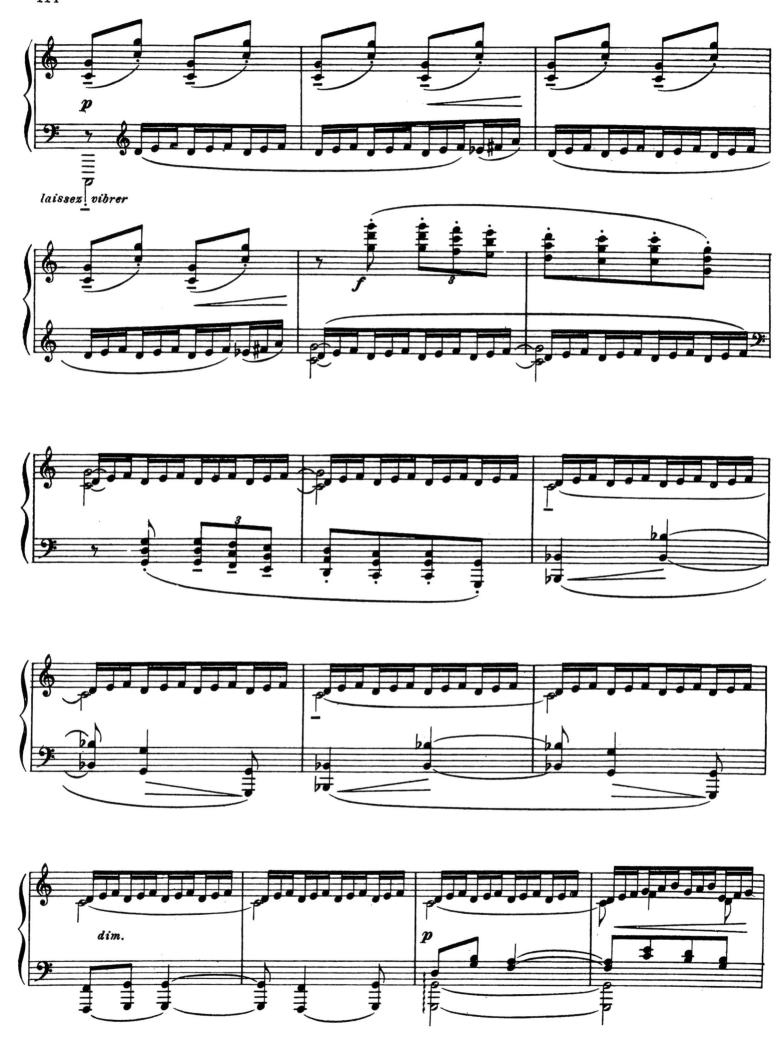

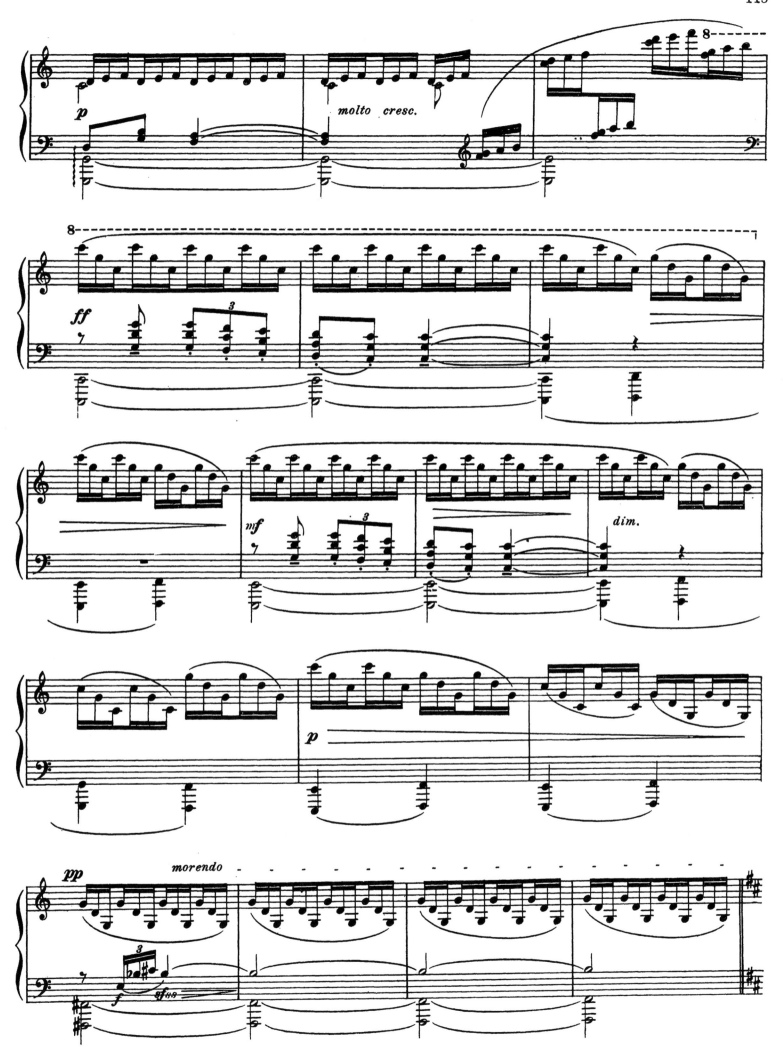

Toutes les notes marquées du signe — sonores, sans dureté,
le reste très léger mais sans sécheresse.

ppp

pp

ppp

un peu en dehors

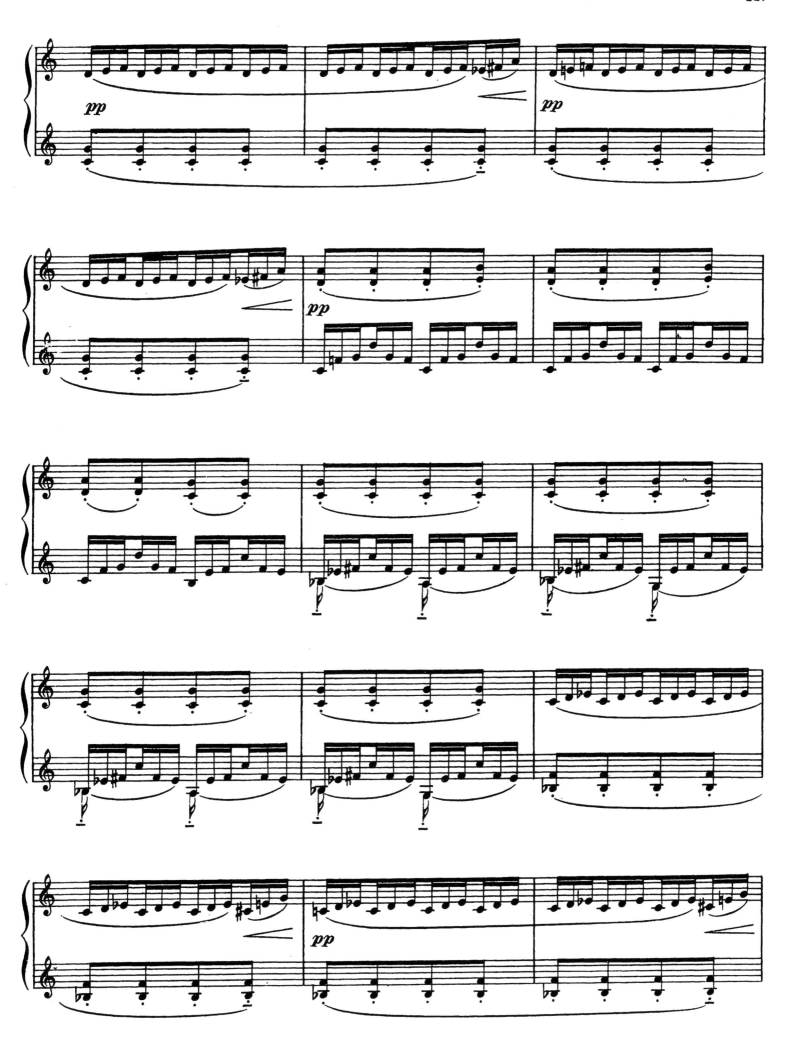

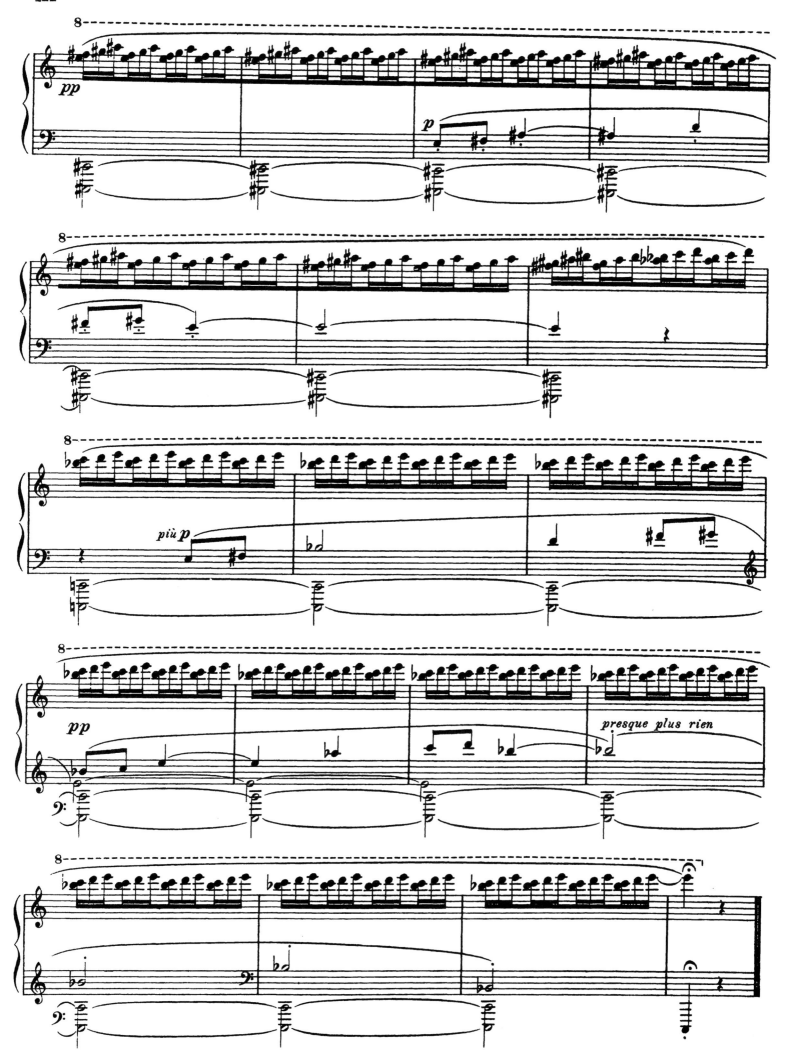

L'APRES-MIDI D'UN FAUNE
(The Afternoon Of A Faun)

CLAUDE DEBUSSY

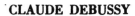

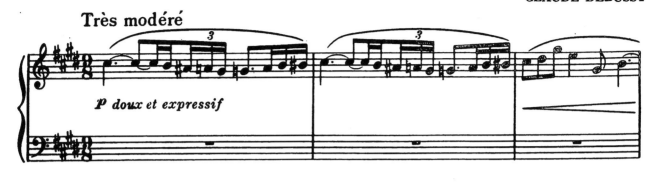

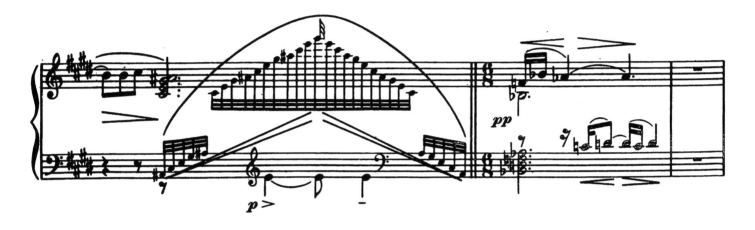

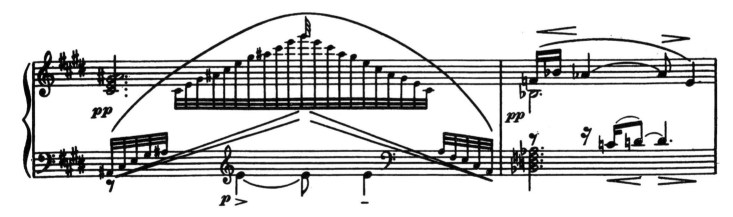

Sole Distributor: **ASHLEY DEALERS SERVICE, INC.**, 263 Veterans Blvd., Carlstadt, N.J. 07072

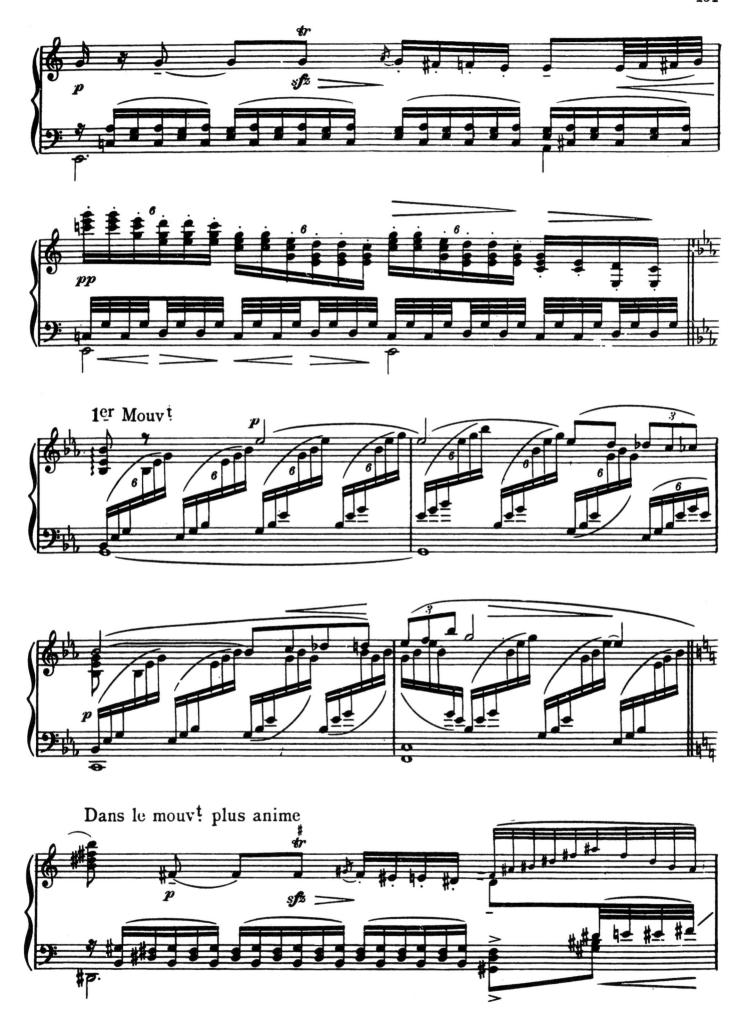

Dans le 1er Mouv^t avec plus de langueur

MASQUES

CLAUDE DEBUSSY

Tres vif et fantasque

laissez vibrer pendant ces 4 mesures

L'ISLE JOYEUSE
(The Happy Island)

CLAUDE DEBUSSY

un peu en dehors
(somewhat marked)

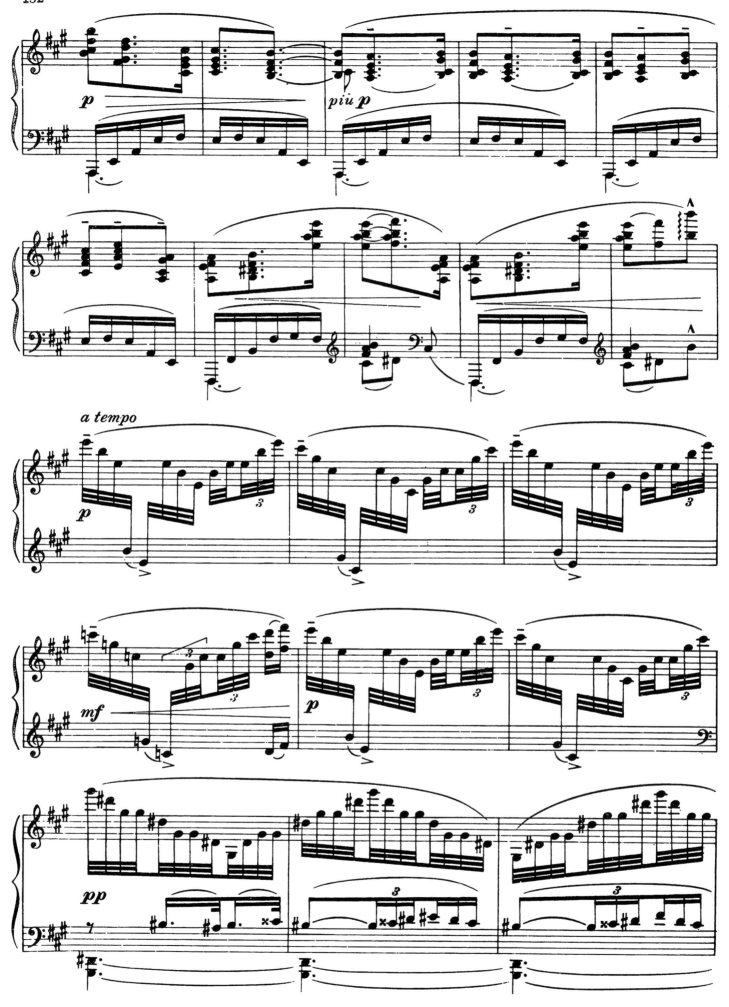

très animé jusqu'à la fin
(very animated to the end)